MOTOCROSS
RACING

BY JACK DAVID

TORQUE™

BELLWETHER MEDIA • MINNEAPOLIS, MN

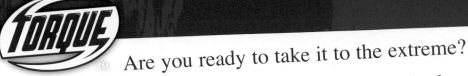

Are you ready to take it to the extreme?
Torque books thrust you into the action-packed world
of sports, vehicles, and adventure. These books may
include dirt, smoke, fire, and dangerous stunts.
WARNING: read at your own risk.

This edition first published in 2008 by Bellwether Media.

No part of this publication may be reproduced in whole or in part without written
permission of the publisher. For information regarding permission, write to Bellwether
Media Inc., Attention: Permissions Department, Post Office Box 1C, Minnetonka, MN
55345-9998.

Library of Congress Cataloging-in-Publication Data
David, Jack, 1968-
  Motocross racing / by Jack David.
      p. cm. -- (Torque. Action sports)
  Summary: "Photographs of amazing feats accompany engaging information about
motocross racing. The combination of high-interest subject matter and light text is
intended to engage readers in grades 3 through 7"--Provided by publisher.
  Includes bibliographical references and index.
  ISBN-13: 978-1-60014-124-9 (hardcover : alk. paper)
  ISBN-10: 1-60014-124-2 (hardcover : alk. paper)
  1. Motocross--Juvenile literature. I. Title.

  GV1060.12.D37 2008
  796.7'56--dc22   2007016794

CONTENTS

THE RACE BEGINS

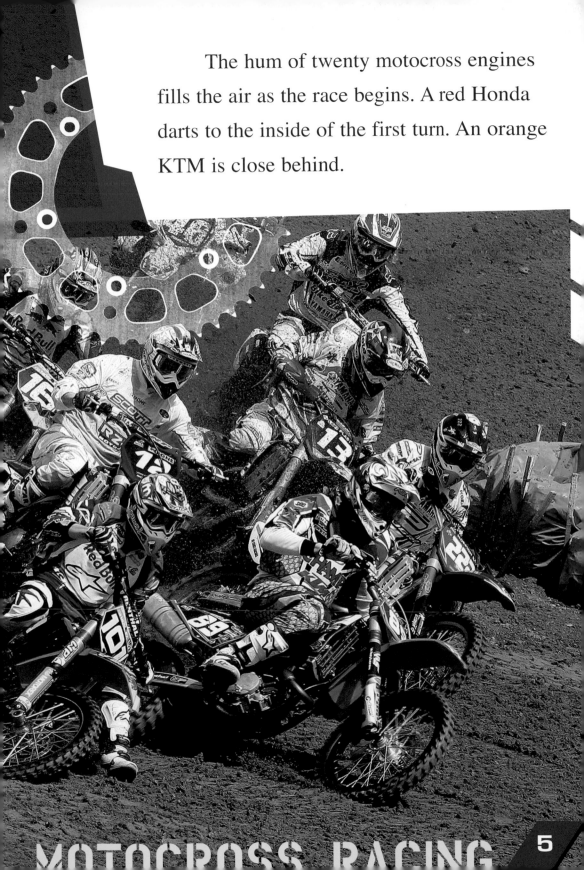

The hum of twenty motocross engines fills the air as the race begins. A red Honda darts to the inside of the first turn. An orange KTM is close behind.

The riders speed to the first jump. Their dirt bikes sail through the air. The rider of the red Honda misjudges the landing. His bike sails too far! He cannot turn smoothly into the next corner. The orange KTM speeds by and takes the lead. A big pack of riders is close behind.

Fast Fact

Most motocross courses are 1 to 2 miles (1.6-3.2 km) long. Riders may race a set amount of laps or a set amount of time.

WHAT IS MOTOCROSS?

Motocross is one of the most popular motor sports in the world. Riders race dirt bikes on outdoor courses with bumps, jumps, and sharp turns. **Supercross** is a sport closely related to motocross. Supercross riders race on smaller indoor courses.

Motocross racing emerged in the 1950s. It grew out of early dirt bike races called **scrambles**. Motocross bikes became faster and more durable than these early dirt bikes. They could speed around a track, sail through the air, and stand up to tough landings. The new sport exploded in popularity.

//TODAY//

//1950//

fast fact

Some riders do tricks
as they sail over jumps.
These tricks helped start
a new sport called
motocross freestyle.

Motocross bikes are built for rough off-road racing. They are light and fast. They have strong springs and shock absorbers to stand up to hard landings. Their tires have deep **tread** to give them a good grip on the loose dirt.

Motocross bikes are grouped by engine size. Engine size is measured in cubic centimeters (cc). Small beginner bikes have engines as small as 50cc. Professional riders often race bikes with 125cc or 250cc engines.

Motocross racing is dangerous. Riders take steps to keep safe during races. They wear full-face helmets, gloves, leather boots, and special clothing. Underneath their clothing they wear **body armor** made of plastic and foam. The body armor protects riders if a bike comes down on top of them.

A motocross event is called a **moto**.
A moto includes several races called **heats**.
The early heats are qualifying races. The
top finishers of each heat advance to the
final. The final heat determines the winner.

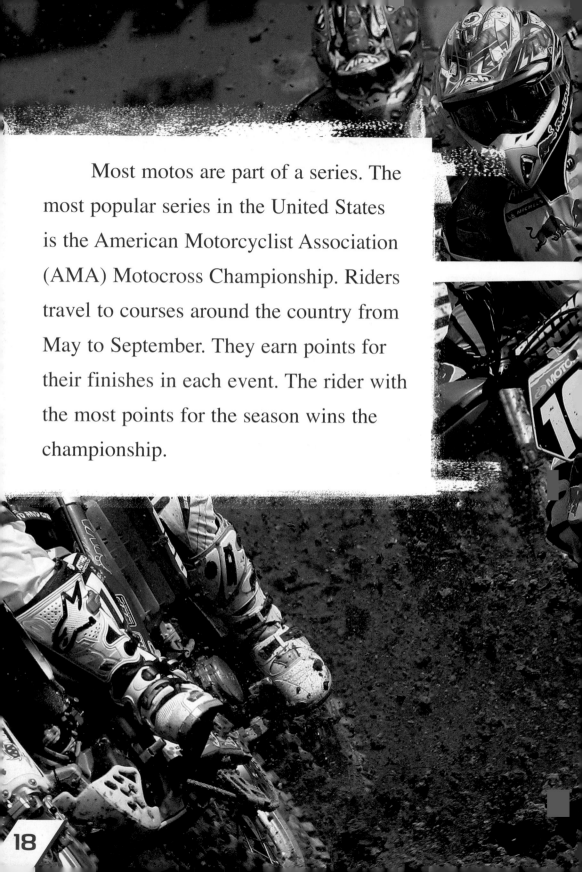

Most motos are part of a series. The most popular series in the United States is the American Motorcyclist Association (AMA) Motocross Championship. Riders travel to courses around the country from May to September. They earn points for their finishes in each event. The rider with the most points for the season wins the championship.

Fast Fact

AMA Motocross Championship riders earn points based on their finishes. Here are the totals:

Finishing Position // Points

1st // 25	8th // 13	15th // 6
2nd // 22	9th // 12	16th // 5
3rd // 20	10th // 11	17th // 4
4th // 18	11th // 10	18th // 3
5th // 16	12th // 9	19th // 2
6th // 15	13th // 8	20th // 1
7th // 14	14th // 7	

Motocross racing is an exciting sport. Huge jumps, intense racing, and thrilling wipeouts provide plenty of action to entertain fans.

GLOSSARY

body armor—a strong piece of plastic and foam that motocross riders wear underneath their clothes to protect them during crashes

heat—an individual motocross race

moto—a single motocross event

scramble—the name given to the earliest dirt bike races

supercross—a sport similar to motocross in which riders race dirt bikes on indoor courses

tread—the series of bumps and grooves on a tire that help it grip rough surfaces

TO LEARN MORE

AT THE LIBRARY

David, Jack. *Moto-X Freestyle*. Minneapolis, Minn.: Bellwether Media, 2008.

Freeman, Gary. *Motocross*. Chicago, Ill.: Heinemann Library, 2003.

Levy, Janey. *Motocross Races*. New York: PowerKids Press, 2007.

ON THE WEB

Learning more about motocross racing is as easy as 1, 2, 3.

1. Go to www.factsurfer.com
2. Enter "motocross racing" into search box.
3. Click the "Surf" button and you will see a list of related web sites.

With factsurfer.com, finding more information is just a click away.

INDEX

The photographs in this book are reproduced through the courtesy of: Juan Martinez, front cover; KTM Sportmotorcycle AG, pp. 2, 4-5, 6-7, 8-9, 16, 18-19, 20-21; Kawasaki Motors Corporation, p. 10; Sherman/Three Lions/Getty Images, p. 11; Suzuki Motor Corporation, pp. 12-13; Ellis Neel, Associated Press, pp. 14-15; Larry Lawrence, p.17.